Your Free

I wanted to show my appreciation that you support my work so I've put together a free gift for you.

TOP 10 RECIPES
Marinades , Sauces, Rubs and Glazes for meat only

http://vasilisabooks.com/freemarinadesfishbook-2/

Just visit the link above to download it now.

I know you will love this gift.

Thanks!

Randy Oliver

Table of Contents

Table of Contents 2

Introduction 5

Garlic Soy Sauce Marinade Salmon 6

Delicious Salmon Marinade 8

Mustard Marinade Baked Fish 10

Marinated Grilled Salmon 12

Orange Marmalade Marinated Salmon 14

Beer & Lime Marinated Salmon 17

Marinated Tuna Steaks 19

Italian Marinated Grilled Swordfish 21

Marinated Mediterranean Fish Fillets 23

Citrus Marinated Swordfish 25

Ginger Marinated Tuna Steaks 27

Grilled Marinated Salmon 29

Lime Soy Ginger Marinated Shrimp 31

Greek-Style Marinated Mahi Mahi 33

Marinated Salmon Seared in a Pepper Crust 35

Honey & Mustard Marinated Salmon 37

Smoked Salmon & Artichoke Dip 40

Marinated Salmon Fillet 42

Marinated and Sautéed Fish 44

Five Spice Marinated Salmon 46

Marinated Seafood Skewers With a Dipping Sauce 48

Ginger Marinated Tuna With Wasabi Butter 51

Rosemary Marinated Tuna 53

Red Snapper or Fresh Tuna Marinating Sauce 55

Marinated Shrimp 57

Marinated Cocktail Shrimp 59

Marinated Shrimp With Capers and Dill 61

Marinated Prawns 63

Spicy Marinated Shrimp 65

Tamari Lemon Marinated Fish 67

Red Snapper with Sesame Ginger Marinade 69

Salmon Marinade 71

Grilled Salmon With Kiwi-Herb Marinade 73

Honey Teriyaki Salmon 75

Teriyaki Tuna With Wasabi Mayonnaise & Pickled Ginger 77

Baked or Grilled Black Cod Teriyaki 79

Grilled Salmon Montreal 81

Chipotle Lime Tuna 83

Grilled Marinated Salmon Fillet 85

Asian Marinated Grilled Tuna 87

Marinated Tuna With Cherry Sauce..89

Marinated Shrimp..91

Delicious Marinated Shrimp 93

Tempting Marinated Shrimp..95

Spicy Marinated Shrimp & Garlic..97

Pepper & Vanilla-Marinated Shrimp..99

Indian Grilled Sour Cream Marinated Shrimp.......................................101

Ginger-Soy-Lime Marinated Shrimp 103

Sweet-N-Spicy Marinated Shrimp..105

Serve immediatelyMarinated Grilled Shrimp 106

Introduction

Almost everyone likes fish, and if you have got a marinade which you make quite easily, it's pretty easy to prepare the fish on the grill.

Boost the tastes of fish with a marinade that goes together in a couple of minutes. This is one of the easiest & tastiest fish marinades that you can ever make! The marinade is best on mahi mahi, or halibut

Fish marinades include a lot of citrus flavors and fresh herbs. Before you cook, grill or bake the fish; just let your fish rest in the marinade for a couple of minutes or hours and it would boost the flavor.

With these marinade recipes, you don't need to worry about the taste; let your refrigerator do the magic for you. Try this once and I bet you would keep trying these recipes for the rest of your life.

The best part about marinades is that it just needs a couple of ingredients that are easily available in the market these days. Season your marinades with more than just white sugar and table salt. Try fish sauce, Worcestershire, soy sauce, mustard, honey, or fruit juice.

You may also brush the reserved marinades on the fish before you tossing them on the hot grill.

Garlic Soy Sauce Marinade Salmon

Nutrition Info (Estimated Amount Per Serving)
317.2 Calories
117 Calories from Fat
13 g Total Fat
1.5 g Saturated Fat
88.4 mg Cholesterol
1120.7 mg Sodium
12.6 g Total Carbohydrate
0.3 g Dietary Fiber
9.9 g Sugars
36.3 g Protein

Total Preparation & Cooking Time: 40 Minutes
Total Servings: 04

Ingredients:
- 1 and 1/2 pounds salmon
- 2 tbsp. canola oil
- 1 cup orange juice

- 2 tbsp. gingerroot, minced
- 1 tbsp. honey
- ¼ cup soy sauce
- 1 clove garlic, minced
- Salt & pepper to taste

Cooking Directions:
1. Combine everything together in a medium size bowl; mix well.
2. Add in the salmon & let it marinate for a minimum period of 15 minutes to an hour.
3. Grill the salmon for 3 to 4 minutes per side, until cooked through.

Delicious Salmon Marinade

Nutrition Info (Estimated Amount Per Serving)
535.6 Calories
247 Calories from Fat
27.5 g Total Fat
4.5 g Saturated Fat
146.3 mg Cholesterol
994.3 mg Sodium
1.7 g Total Carbohydrate
0.3 g Dietary Fiber
0.4 g Sugars
66.8 g Protein

Total Preparation & Cooking Time: 40 Minutes
Total Servings: 05

Ingredients:
- 4 salmon steaks or salmon fillets
- 2 green onions or 2 scallions, chopped
- 1 clove garlic, chopped finely
- 3 tbsp. soy sauce

- 2 tsp. ginger, fresh, peeled & chopped finely
- ¼ cup olive oil

Cooking Directions:
1. Mix scallions together with the soy sauce, oil, ginger, and garlic; mix well and make a marinade in a medium size bowl.
2. Add in the salmon; turn to coat with the marinade, preferably several times and let the salmon marinate for an hour in a refrigerator or fridge.
3. Grill the salmon until it flakes, when pierced with a fork, for 3 to 4 minutes per side.

Mustard Marinade Baked Fish

Nutrition Info (Estimated Amount Per Serving)
156.2 Calories
16 Calories from Fat
1.8 g Total Fat
0.3 g Saturated Fat
73.1 mg Cholesterol
272.7 mg Sodium
2.7 g Total Carbohydrate
0.8 g Dietary Fiber
0.8 g Sugars
31.1 g Protein

Total Preparation & Cooking Time: 45 Minutes
Total Servings: 05

Ingredients:
- 1 and 1/2 pounds cod or haddock or scrod fish or any white fish fillets (rinse & dry)
- 1/4 cup Dijon mustard, coarse or smooth
- 2 tsp. zest of lemon, grated
- 1/2 tsp. thyme, dried

- 1 to 2 tsp. horseradish, prepared
- 1/3 cup lemon juice, fresh
- 1/4 tsp. black pepper, ground

Cooking Directions:
1. Whirl all of the marinade ingredients together in a small food processor or blender or whisk them in a mixing bowl.
2. Place the fish fillets in a baking pan, preferably lightly oiled & skin side down.
3. Transfer the marinade at the top of the fish; turn the fillets several times until both sides are evenly coated with the marinade.
4. Let the fillets marinate in a refrigerator for a minimum period of 20 minutes to an hour.
5. Preheat your oven to 400 F/205C in advance.
6. Place the baking dish in the oven, preferably uncovered & bake until the fish flakes easily with a fork and become tender, for 10 to 15 minutes.

Marinated Grilled Salmon

Nutrition Info (Estimated Amount Per Serving)
407.4 Calories
174 Calories from Fat
19.3 g Total Fat
2.8 g Saturated Fat
87.5 mg Cholesterol
1288.4 mg Sodium
23.6 g Total Carbohydrate
0.3 g Dietary Fiber
19.7 g Sugars
35.7 g Protein

Total Preparation & Cooking Time: 15 Minutes
Total Servings: 04

Ingredients:
- 4 salmon fillets, 1" thick (approximately 6 oz.)

For Sauce

- Cream cheese
- Reserved marinade

For Marinade
- ¼ cup honey
- ¼ cup mango chutney
- 2 cloves garlic, minced finely
- ¼ cup soy sauce
- ¼ cup lemon or lime juice
- ¼ cup Worcestershire sauce
- 1 tsp. dill
- ¼ cup olive oil

Cooking Directions:
1. Mix all of the marinade ingredients together in a plastic bag, preferably large size; mix well and then add in the salmon fillets. Let the fillets to marinate for 6 to 8 hrs in a refrigerator.
2. While you grill the salmon, transfer the marinade to a saucepan, preferably small size; pressing through a sieve.
3. Grill over low to medium heat settings and add in the cream cheese & add it into the sauce until you get your preferred consistency.

Orange Marmalade Marinated Salmon

Nutrition Info (Estimated Amount Per Serving)
530 Calories
133 Calories from Fat
14.8 g Total Fat
2.6 g Saturated Fat
130.7 mg Cholesterol
1582.7 mg Sodium
37.5 g Total Carbohydrate
0.7 g Dietary Fiber
32.7 g Sugars
61 g Protein

Total Preparation & Cooking Time: 15 Minutes
Total Servings: 04

Ingredients:

- 2 and 1/2 pounds salmon fillets, fresh, washed & towel dried
- 1 tsp. garlic, minced
- 2/3 cup orange marmalade
- 1 tsp. ginger, fresh & grated
- 2 tsp. onion flakes, dried
- 1/3 cup rice vinegar
- 1 tsp. sesame oil
- 1/3 cup soy sauce
- 1 tsp. olive oil
- Pepper to taste
- 1 pinch chili pepper flakes
- Scallion, fresh & sliced to garnish

Cooking Directions:
1. Combine orange marmalade together with the soy sauce, rice vinegar, grated fresh ginger, minced garlic, onion flakes; sesame oil & olive oil in a zip lock gallon size bag; mix well.
2. Seal & mash until well blended, preferably using your hands.
3. Add in the Salmon and allow it to marinate for an hour.
4. Heat a grill in advance, preferably over medium to high heat settings.
5. Lightly spray a heavy duty foil or fish basket with the nonstick oil, if using.
6. Remove the salmon from marinade & reserve. Place salmon into foil folding tail or basket to make it even thickness.
7. Place wrapped in foil or basket on barbecue & grill the salmon for 5 to 7 minutes, preferably skin side up.
8. In the meantime, bring the marinade to a boil and then decrease the heat settings and let it simmer until fish is completely cooked.
9. Turn the basket over & grill the salmon for 5 to 7 more minutes, until just opaque in the middle.
10. Turn the salmon out onto a platter.

11. Drizzle the salmon with the reduced marinade & garnish it with the scallions.

Beer & Lime Marinated Salmon

Nutrition Info (Estimated Amount Per Serving)
169.1 Calories
45 Calories from Fat
5 g Total Fat
0.9 g Saturated Fat
52.3 mg Cholesterol
841 mg Sodium
3.6 g Total Carbohydrate
0.3 g Dietary Fiber
0.7 g Sugars
25 g Protein

Total Preparation & Cooking Time: 20 Minutes
Total Servings: 04

Ingredients:
- 1 pound salmon fillet, fresh
- 3 tbsp. soy sauce

- 1/2 tbsp. gingerroot, fresh & minced
- 2 garlic cloves, minced
- 1/3 cup beer
- 2 tbsp. red or green or yellow bell peppers, finely diced (or combo)
- 1/4 cup lime juice, fresh
- Zest of 2 to 3 limes or 2 tbsp.
- Black pepper, fresh ground to taste

Cooking Directions:
1. Mix lime juice together with the soy sauce, beer, garlic, and ginger; mix well.
2. Place the salmon fillets, preferably in a shallow glass dish & pour the marinade over it; turning the fillets several times until well coated with the mixture; cover & let refrigerate for overnight.
3. Preheat the grill in advance.
4. Remove the fillets from marinade; discarding the marinade.
5. Grill until fish flakes in center, for 10 to 12 minutes.
6. Garnish the cooked fillets with lime zest, diced bell pepper & pepper over the top. Serve warm.

Marinated Tuna Steaks

Nutrition Info (Estimated Amount Per Serving)
409.7 Calories
166 Calories from Fat
18.5 g Total Fat
3.5 g Saturated Fat
64.6 mg Cholesterol
1075.9 mg Sodium
3.7 g Total Carbohydrate
0.2 g Dietary Fiber
1 g Sugars
41.7 g Protein

Total Preparation & Cooking Time: 20 Minutes
Total Servings: 04

Ingredients:
- 4 tuna steaks, preferably 1" thick (approximately 6 oz.)
- 1 tbsp. lemon juice
- 1/4 cup sherry, dry

- 1 tsp. lemon zest
- ¼ cup soy sauce
- 1 clove garlic, crushed
- Black pepper, ground to taste
- 3 tbsp. olive oil

Cooking Directions:
1. Mix soy together with the sherry, lemon zest, juice, garlic & olive oil in a medium size bowl.
2. Add the steaks and let marinate in the mixture for an hour; turning several times to coat.
3. Lift the steaks from marinade, when you are ready to cook them and sprinkle black pepper over the top.
4. Barbeque the steaks until you get your desired doneness, for a couple of minutes on both sides. Make sure that you don't over-cook them.

Italian Marinated Grilled Swordfish

Nutrition Info (Estimated Amount Per Serving)
448.2 Calories
325 Calories from Fat
36.1 g Total Fat
6 g Saturated Fat
89.8 mg Cholesterol
694.5 mg Sodium
3 g Total Carbohydrate
0.4 g Dietary Fiber
1.4 g Sugars
27 g Protein

Total Preparation & Cooking Time: 25 Minutes
Total Servings: 02

Ingredients:
- 2 swordfish steaks, sliced; preferably 1" thick
- 1 tsp. thyme, fresh & chopped
- 1 tbsp. balsamic vinegar
- 1 tsp. sage, fresh & finely chopped
- 1 tbsp. lemon juice
- 1 clove garlic, minced
- 1 tsp. rosemary, fresh & chopped
- 3 + 1 tbsp. of olive oil
- Salt & black pepper, freshly ground to taste

Cooking Directions:
1. Combine 3 tbs. olive oil together with everything else (except the steaks) in a bowl, preferably small size; mix well.
2. Place the steaks of swordfish in a bag, preferably zip-lock; unsealed.
3. Pour the marinade into the same zip lock bag; toss the fish until completely coated with the marinade; preferably using your fingers.
4. Seal the bag & release as much air as you possibly can.
5. Let the steaks marinate in a refrigerator for a minimum of 3 to 4 hrs.
6. Preheat the grill in advance, preferably over medium to high heat settings.
7. Brush the grill rack with the leftover tbsp. of olive oil, once it's searing hot.
8. Grill until the fish flakes easily when forked and the center of the steaks are cooked through, for 3 to 5 minutes per side.

Marinated Mediterranean Fish Fillets

Nutrition Info (Estimated Amount Per Serving)
185.8 Calories
33 Calories from Fat
3.8 g Total Fat
0.6 g Saturated Fat
82.5 mg Cholesterol
119.4 mg Sodium
1.8 g Total Carbohydrate
0.5 g Dietary Fiber
0.3 g Sugars
34.6 g Protein

Total Preparation & Cooking Time: 45 Minutes
Total Servings: 06

Ingredients:
- 6 fish fillets, (approximately ¼ pounds)
- 3 tsp. olive oil

For Marinade:
- 2 tsp. paprika
- 3 tbsp. lemon juice
- 2 tbsp. coriander leaves, fresh & chopped
- 3 cloves garlic, crushed
- 2 tbsp. parsley, fresh & chopped
- 1 tsp. cumin, ground
- 1/2 tsp. black pepper, freshly ground
- Cayenne pepper to taste

Cooking Directions:
1. Combine all of the marinade ingredients together in a medium-size bowl. Add in the fillets and let marinade for a minimum period of half an hour or little more.
2. Heat oil in a non-stick frying pan, preferably over moderate heat settings. Remove the fillets from marinade and fry the fish until cooked through.

Citrus Marinated Swordfish

Nutrition Info (Estimated Amount Per Serving)
420.1 Calories
292 Calories from Fat
32.5 g Total Fat
5.2 g Saturated Fat
53 mg Cholesterol
128.1 mg Sodium
4.4 g Total Carbohydrate
0.6 g Dietary Fiber
0.8 g Sugars
27.6 g Protein

Total Preparation & Cooking Time: 01 Hr & 30 Minutes
Total Servings: 06

Ingredients:
- 4 swordfish steaks, medium (approximately ¾" thick)
- Zest of 1 lime, medium & grated
- 1 bunch cilantro, fresh & chopped
- 6 cloves garlic, minced
- Juice of 3 limes, medium
- 3 Serrano chilies, small & chopped
- 1/2 cup olive oil

Cooking Directions:
1. Place everything together in a Ziploc bag, preferably large size (including the swordfish steaks) for a minimum period of an hour or for overnight in a refrigerator.
2. Preheat the grill in advance, preferably on high heat settings & for a minimum period of 10 minutes.
3. Cook the steaks until flaky in the middle, for 5 to 6 minutes each side.

Ginger Marinated Tuna Steaks

Nutrition Info (Estimated Amount Per Serving)
286.2 Calories
105 Calories from Fat
11.8 g Total Fat
2.6 g Saturated Fat
64.6 mg Cholesterol
598.1 mg Sodium
2 g Total Carbohydrate
0.2 g Dietary Fiber
0.3 g Sugars
40.6 g Protein

Total Preparation & Cooking Time: 55 Minutes
Total Servings: 04

Ingredients:
- 4 tuna steaks, fresh, 1" thick, rinsed & patted dry (approximately 6 oz.)

- 1 clove garlic, minced
- 2 tbsp. rice vinegar
- 1 tbsp. ginger, fresh & grated
- 1/4 cup soy sauce, reduced sodium
- 1 tbsp. sesame oil, dark
- 1 tbsp. onion, green & sliced

Cooking Directions:
1. Combine everything together (except the tuna) in a small bowl.
2. Place the tuna steaks in a plastic bag, preferably zip lock type. Pour the marinade over the bag with tuna and seal; setting the bag in a shallow pan.
3. Let it refrigerate for a minimum of half an hour, turning the bag several times to coat the tuna with the marinade.
4. Using nonstick cooking spray, lightly coat the grill rack.
5. Drain the tuna; discarding the marinade.
6. Grill fish until it flakes with a fork, for 10 to 12 minutes, turning once during the cooking.

Grilled Marinated Salmon

Nutrition Info (Estimated Amount Per Serving)
359.5 Calories
122 Calories from Fat
13.6 g Total Fat
2.3 g Saturated Fat
104.6 mg Cholesterol
1176.4 mg Sodium
8.1 g Total Carbohydrate
0.4 g Dietary Fiber
6.7 g Sugars
48.7 g Protein

Total Preparation & Cooking Time: 20 Minutes
Total Servings: 04

Ingredients:
- 2 pounds salmon fillets
- 1 tsp. mustard powder

- 1/4 cup soy sauce
- 1 tsp. ginger, grounded
- 1/4 cup rice wine vinegar
- 1 tsp. black pepper, grounded
- 2 tbsp. white sugar
- 1 tbsp. vegetable oil

Cooking Directions:

1. Combine soy sauce together with the sugar, vinegar, mustard powder, ground black pepper, ginger and oil in a medium size bowl.
2. Place the salmon fillets in a shallow dish, preferably nonporous & transfer the marinade at the top of the salmon. Cover & let the fish to marinate in a refrigerator for a minimum period of an hour, turning every now and then.
3. Preheat an outdoor grill in advance, preferably over medium to high heat settings and oil the grate lightly.
4. Grill the fish until you get your desired doneness, for 3 to 4 minutes per side.

Lime Soy Ginger Marinated Shrimp

Nutrition Info (Estimated Amount Per Serving)
236.2 Calories
95 Calories from Fat
10.6 g Total Fat
1.7 g Saturated Fat
191 mg Cholesterol
2871.3 mg Sodium
10.6 g Total Carbohydrate
0.6 g Dietary Fiber
4.2 g Sugars
24.9 g Protein

Total Preparation & Cooking Time: 30 Minutes
Total Servings: 06

Ingredients:
- 2 pounds shrimp, large, shells & tails on
- 3/4 cup soy sauce

- 2 shallots, large, peeled & chopped
- 1/4 cup green onion, chopped
- 1 and 1/2 tbsp. sugar
- 1/4 cup peanut or olive oil
- 4 cloves garlic, minced or smashed
- 1/2 cup lime juice, fresh
- 1 to 2 tbsp. ginger, fresh, peeled & chopped
- 1/4 tsp. black pepper, fresh & coarsely grounded or to taste

Cooking Directions:

1. Place shallots together with the garlic, ginger, lime juice, soy, & sugar in a high-speed blender & blend on high settings until smooth.
2. Add in the oil and green onion; blend again until well combined. Season the mixture with black pepper.
3. Arrange the shrimp in a bowl, preferably large size & pour the marinade over them. Let marinate for a minimum period of 20 minutes to an hour, preferably at room temperature.
4. Preheat a grill in advance, preferably over high heat settings. Remove the shrimp from marinade & grill for a minute or two per side.

Greek-Style Marinated Mahi Mahi

Nutrition Info (Estimated Amount Per Serving)
372.2 Calories
252 Calories from Fat
28.1 g Total Fat
4 g Saturated Fat
103.4 mg Cholesterol
272.4 mg Sodium
3.8 g Total Carbohydrate
0.8 g Dietary Fiber
0.8 g Sugars
26.6 g Protein

Total Preparation & Cooking Time: 20 Minutes
Total Servings: 04

Ingredients:

- 1 and 1⁄4 pounds mahi mahi fillets, thawed or fresh, approximately 3/4 to 1" thick; rinse & pat dry using paper towels; cut into 4 serving size pieces
- 3 tbsp. oregano, fresh & chopped
- 1⁄2 cup lemon juice
- 1 tsp. garlic, bottled & minced
- 3 tbsp. mint, fresh & chopped
- 1⁄2 cup olive oil
- 1 tsp. lemon peel, finely shredded (zest)
- 1⁄4 tsp. salt

Cooking Directions:
1. Place the fish in a plastic bag, preferably reseal able. Stir lemon juice together with the mint, oregano, olive oil, lemon zest, garlic & salt; mix well. Pour the marinade over the fish. Seal the bag & turn several times to coat. Marinate in a refrigerator for a minimum period of half an hour.
2. Drain the fish; reserve the marinade.
3. Grill until fish flakes easily when tested with a fork, for 8 to 12 minutes, preferably over medium heat settings, turning once & brushing with the marinade halfway during grilling; discarding any leftover marinade.

Marinated Salmon Seared in a Pepper Crust

Nutrition Info (Estimated Amount Per Serving)
369.7 Calories
190 Calories from Fat
21.2 g Total Fat
3.3 g Saturated Fat
78.4 mg Cholesterol
1134.9 mg Sodium
6.9 g Total Carbohydrate
1.4 g Dietary Fiber
2.6 g Sugars
37.4 g Protein

Total Preparation & Cooking Time: 45 Minutes
Total Servings: 02

Ingredients:
- 3/4 pound salmon fillet
- 1 clove garlic, pressed
- 2 tsp. lemon juice, fresh

- 4 tsp. pepper
- 2 tbsp. olive oil
- 1 tsp. sugar
- 2 tbsp. soy sauce

Cooking Directions:
1. Combine soy sauce together with the lemon juice, garlic, & sugar in a plastic bag, preferably sealable; mix the ingredients well, add then add in the salmon. Turn several times to coat it well
2. Let it marinate for half an hour, preferably sealed & chilled.
3. Remove the salmon; discarding the marinade, pat it dry & press 2 tsp. of pepper onto every salmon piece, coat it carefully.
4. Heat the oil over moderate to high heat settings in a heavy skillet until very hot but ensure that it's not smoky. Sauté the salmon until it just flakes or for 2 minutes on each side.
5. Using a slotted spatula, transfer the salmon to paper towels & let drain for half a minute.

Honey & Mustard Marinated Salmon

Nutrition Info (Estimated Amount Per Serving)
748.8 Calories
328 Calories from Fat
36.5 g Total Fat
11.2 g Saturated Fat
135.1 mg Cholesterol
369.1 mg Sodium
61.4 g Total Carbohydrate
9.8 g Dietary Fiber
46.9 g Sugars
48.7 g Protein

Total Preparation & Cooking Time: 01 Hr & 05 Minutes
Total Servings: 02

Ingredients:
- 1 pound salmon fillet, pin bones removed, skin on, rinsed under cold running water & pat dry using paper towels

- 2 tbsp. olive oil
- 1 tbsp. honey
- 2 tbsp. Dijon mustard
- 1 clove garlic, minced
- 1 tbsp. lemon juice, fresh
- 1 tsp. chili powder
- Salt, to taste

For Apples
- 4 Golden Delicious sweet apples
- 2 tbsp. butter, unsalted
- 1 sprig of rosemary, fresh
- Mint leaves, fresh to garnish

Cooking Directions:
1. Place the fillets in a shallow dish.
2. Mix olive oil together with mustard, honey, garlic, chili powder, and lemon juice in a measuring cup; pour the mixture over salmon; turn several times until well coated with the mixture.
3. Cover and let marinade for a minimum period of half an hour at room temperature or place it in a refrigerator for 2 to 3 hours; turning once or twice.
4. Preheat your oven to 190 C/375 F in advance. Reserve the marinade & transfer the salmon to a baking dish.
5. Place the dish with salmon in the preheated oven and let the salmon bake for 6 to 8 minutes; transfer the marinade at the top of the salmon.
6. Continue cooking until the salmon flakes easily with a fork, for 4 to 5 more minutes; season the cooked salmon with salt.
7. While you cook the salmon, core and cut each apple into wedges, preferably 8.
8. Over medium to high heat settings in a large and heavy skillet; heat the butter until completely melt.
9. Add the rosemary and apples; decrease the heat settings to medium and cook until tender, for 4 to 5 minutes.

10. Remove from heat; discarding the rosemary.
11. Serve the salmon with pan drippings spoon over & top it with the apples. If desired, feel free to garnish it with fresh mint leaves.

Smoked Salmon & Artichoke Dip

Nutrition Info (Estimated Amount Per Serving)
138.3 Calories
74 Calories from Fat
8.3 g Total Fat
3 g Saturated Fat
19.2 mg Cholesterol
532.5 mg Sodium
8.7 g Total Carbohydrate
2.7 g Dietary Fiber
1.7 g Sugars
8.6 g Protein

Total Preparation & Cooking Time: 35 Minutes
Total Servings: 08

Ingredients:
- 6 ounces sea bear northwest salmon, smoked, drained, skin removed & break into 1/2" small chunks
- 2 jars marinated artichoke hearts, drain and chop (approximately 6 and 1/2 oz.)

- 1 can mild green chilies, drain and chop (approximately 4 oz)
- 3/4 cup cheddar cheese, grated
- 6 tbsp. mayonnaise
- Pepper & salt to taste

Cooking Directions:

1. Mix smoked salmon together with the chilies and artichokes.
2. Reserve a tbsp. of cheese to sprinkle over the top & fold in mayonnaise and the remaining cheese, pepper & salt.
3. Cover & bake in a pre-heated oven at 175 C/350 F until cooked through, for 15 to 20 minutes.

Marinated Salmon Fillet

Nutrition Info (Estimated Amount Per Serving)
155.3 Calories
35 Calories from Fat
4 g Total Fat
0.7 g Saturated Fat
59.1 mg Cholesterol
378 mg Sodium
5.5 g Total Carbohydrate
0.2 g Dietary Fiber
3.6 g Sugars
23.3 g Protein

Total Preparation & Cooking Time: 01 Hr & 20 Minutes
Total Servings: 04

Ingredients:
- 1 pound salmon fillet

- 1 tbsp. lemon juice, fresh
- 2 tbsp. soy sauce, reduced sodium
- 1 tbsp. garlic
- 1 tbsp. brown sugar
- 1 tsp. ginger

Cooking Directions:
1. Place the salmon fillets, preferably skin-side up in a square baking dish of 8".
2. Combine all of the marinade ingredients together in a small bowl and add in the sugar; stir well until completely dissolved.
3. Pour the mixture over salmon; turn the fish several times until coated with the mixture.
4. Using plastic wrap, cover the dish and let chill for an hour.
5. Heat an oven to 375 F/190 C.
6. Replace the plastic wrap with foil and bake until cooked through, for 15 to 20 minutes

Marinated and Sautéed Fish

Nutrition Info (Estimated Amount Per Serving)
642.3 Calories
196 Calories from Fat
21.8 g Total Fat
11.2 g Saturated Fat
210.2 mg Cholesterol
672.7 mg Sodium
44.5 g Total Carbohydrate
3.3 g Dietary Fiber
4.7 g Sugars
51.2 g Protein

Total Preparation & Cooking Time: 35 Minutes
Total Servings: 04

Ingredients:
3 to 4 catfish or flounder fillets

For Marinade
- 1 cup white wine, not too sweet
- Juice of 1 lime, fresh
- 1 tsp. mustard, dry
- 2 cloves garlic, minced
- Salt, lemon pepper & other herbs or seasonings to taste

For Breading
- 1 and 1/2 cups breadcrumbs
- 1 egg, medium
- Olive oil
- 1/4 cup butter

Cooking Directions:
1. In a pie plate or glass bowl; mix all of the marinade ingredients together; mix well & then add in the fish fillets. Let the fillets marinate for a minimum period of an hour to 2 hours
2. Add butter together with olive oil in a heavy skillet, preferably over medium heat settings.
3. Beat egg in one bowl & bread crumbs in a separate bowl.
4. Dip fillets in the egg mixture, preferably one at a time and then roll them in the bread crumbs; discarding the marinade.
5. Put the fillets in the skillet, preferably 2 at a time & sauté for 5 minutes; flip and cook the other side for five minutes as well until flake easily with a fork.
6. If you think you need to add more butter, then feel free to add 2 tbsp. of more butter. While cooking, you can even add a splash of wine, if desired.
7. Serve & enjoy!

Five Spice Marinated Salmon

Nutrition Info (Estimated Amount Per Serving)
258.1 Calories
74 Calories from Fat
8.2 g Total Fat
1.3 g Saturated Fat
88.7 mg Cholesterol
874.2 mg Sodium
5.6 g Total Carbohydrate
0.3 g Dietary Fiber
3.6 g Sugars
35.6 g Protein

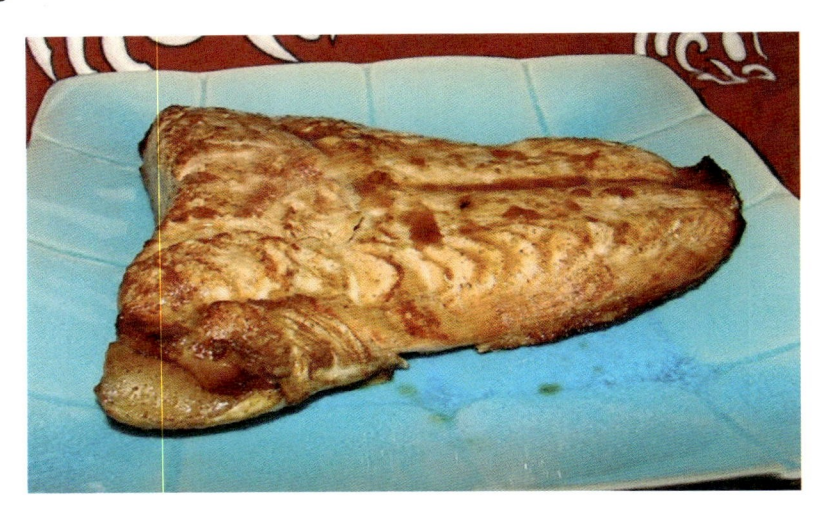

Total Preparation & Cooking Time: 25 Minutes
Total Servings: 04

Ingredients:
- 1 and 1/2 pounds salmon fillet, skinless & cut into 1" strips

For Marinade
- 3 tbsp. soy sauce
- 3 tbsp. Chinese rice wine

- 2 tsp. sesame oil
- 1 tbsp. brown sugar
- 1 tbsp. limes or 1 tablespoon lemon juice
- 1 tsp. Chinese five spice powder
- 2 to 3 dashes of hot pepper sauce or to taste

For Garnish
- Lime or lemons wedge
- 1 tbsp. ginger grated or to taste

Cooking Directions:
1. Mix all of the marinade ingredients together in a zip lock bag or shallow baking dish, preferably nonmetallic.
2. Add the salmon strips; gently turn until coated with the mixture.
3. Refrigerate for half an hour to 6 hours (maximum), turning once or twice.
4. Remove the salmon fillets from marinade; placing them in a casserole dish (you need to be careful here, you need to choose one which would fit inside your bamboo steamer).
5. Brush salmon generously with your desired oriental sauce & sprinkle ginger (grated) over the top of it.
6. Cover with a bamboo lid and place over the boiling water and let steam until fish flakes with a fork, for 10 to 12 minutes.
7. Serve the fillets over rice with lime/lemon wedge

Marinated Seafood Skewers With a Dipping Sauce

Nutrition Info (Estimated Amount Per Serving)
502.8 Calories
122 Calories from Fat
13.6 g Total Fat
2.7 g Saturated Fat
122.9 mg Cholesterol
1810.5 mg Sodium
39.8 g Total Carbohydrate
0.8 g Dietary Fiber
34.6 g Sugars
54.5 g Protein

Total Preparation & Cooking Time: 35 Minutes
Total Servings: 03

Ingredients:
For Marinade

- 3 cloves garlic, crushed
- 3 tbsp. soy sauce
- 1 tsp. fish sauce
- 2 tsp. sesame oil
- 2 tsp. ginger, fresh & grated
- 1 tbsp. ketjap manis
- 2 tsp. sweet chili sauce
- 2 tbsp. lime juice
- 2 tsp. lemongrass chopped finely
- 3 green onions, thinly sliced

For Fish

- 6 long wooden skewers, soaked in water for a minimum period of half an hour before using
- 12 green prawns, peeled
- 320 grams tuna steaks, cut into large cubes
- 340 grams salmon fillets, cut into large cubes

For Dipping Sauce

- 1 and 1/2-2 tbsp. coriander, finely chopped
- 3 tsp. white wine vinegar
- 50 ml lime juice
- 2 tsp. soy sauce
- 1 tsp. fish sauce
- 100 grams sugar
- Zest of 1 lime, small
- 3 tbsp. sweet chili sauce
- 1/2 cup water

Cooking Directions:
1. Combine all of the marinade ingredients together in a storage container or bowl, preferably large size; mix well and then add in the chopped prawns & fish. Let refrigerate for a couple of hours to marinate.
2. Thread the fish onto skewers alternating, prawn, salmon, tuna, etc.; reserving the marinade.

3. Grill & cook until done, for 8 to 10 minutes (about 6" away from the heat source), turning once or twice and during cooking, don't forget to baste with the reserved marinade.
4. For Dipping Sauce; add sugar and water in a saucepan & cook until the sugar completely dissolves, preferably over medium to high heat settings.
5. Decrease the heat settings and then add in lime zest, juice, soy, fish sauce, sweet chili sauce, and vinegar, stir well to combine and remove from the heat, add the coriander; stir well & serve in separate dipping bowls.

Ginger Marinated Tuna With Wasabi Butter

Nutrition Info (Estimated Amount Per Serving)
575.2 Calories
313 Calories from Fat
34.8 g Total Fat
17.2 g Saturated Fat
125.6 mg Cholesterol
1012.7 mg Sodium
13.3 g Total Carbohydrate
0.3 g Dietary Fiber
10.5 g Sugars
41.2 g Protein

Total Preparation & Cooking Time: 01 Hr
Total Servings: 04

Ingredients:
- 4 tuna steaks, washed using cold running water & pat dry (approximately 6 to 8 oz.)
- 2 tbsp. wasabi powder
- 1 tbsp. fresh orange juice
- 1/2 cup butter, unsalted & softened

- 1 tbsp. cilantro, fresh & minced
- 1 tsp. kosher salt

For Marinade
- 1/3 cup rice vinegar
- 3 tbsp. sugar
- 3 tbsp. dry sherry or apple juice
- 2 tbsp. soy sauce
- 1 tbsp. chili-garlic sauce
- 1 tbsp. sesame oil, toasted
- 1/4 cup scallion, chopped
- 4 cloves garlic, peeled
- Fresh gingerroot, preferably 1", peeled & cut into fourths

Cooking Directions:
1. For butter; mix all of the ingredients together (except the tuna steaks and the ingredients for marinade) in a bowl, preferably small size; cover & let refrigerate until ready to serve.
2. Place all of the marinade ingredients together in a jar of high-speed blender and blend on high settings until blended and coarsely chopped.
3. Place the tuna steaks in a shallow container and transfer the prepared marinade over it. Let it marinate for a minimum period of half an hour.
4. Preheat your grill in advance, preferably over medium to high heat settings.
5. Remove tuna from the marinade & to prevent from sticking to grill, don't forget to spray it lightly with a non-stick cooking spray.
6. Place the steaks onto the preheated grill and cook until you get your desired doneness; turning once or twice.
7. Top every cooked steak with 1/2 - 1 tsp. of wasabi butter & serve with more butter on the side.

Rosemary Marinated Tuna

Nutrition Info (Estimated Amount Per Serving)
161.4 Calories
162 Calories from Fat
18 g Total Fat
2.5 g Saturated Fat
0 mg Cholesterol
97.4 mg Sodium
0.7 g Total Carbohydrate
0.1 g Dietary Fiber
0.2 g Sugars
0 g Protein

Total Preparation & Cooking Time: 01 Hr & 10 Minutes
Total Servings: 06

Ingredients:
- 6 tuna steaks (approximately 2 and ½ to 3 pounds)
- 1 bay leaf
- 1⁄4 to 1⁄2 tsp. salt or to taste
- 1⁄2 tsp. rosemary, dried or fresh
- Lemon wedge
- Pepper to taste

- Juice of 1 lemon, fresh
- 1/2 cup olive oil

Cooking Directions:
1. Arrange fish in a shallow pan, preferably in a single layer.
2. Mix everything (except Tuna steaks and Lemon wedge) in a large size bowl; mix well and then transfer the mixture over the steaks. Let the tuna marinate in a refrigerator for an hour, turning once or twice.
3. Grill or Broil the steaks for 4 to 5 minutes per side; basting the steaks with marinade (without the bay leaf).
4. Serve hot with lemon wedges

Red Snapper or Fresh Tuna Marinating Sauce

Nutrition Info (Estimated Amount Per Serving)
210.7 Calories
96 Calories from Fat
10.7 g Total Fat
4.3 g Saturated Fat
54.6 mg Cholesterol
116.7 mg Sodium
0.5 g Total Carbohydrate
0 g Dietary Fiber
0.1 g Sugars
26.6 g Protein

Total Preparation & Cooking Time: 45 Minutes
Total Servings: 16

Ingredients:
- 4 pounds red snapper or tuna, fresh, rinsed & dried well
- 1/4 to 1/2 tsp. black pepper, fresh ground
- 4 tbsp. lemon juice, fresh or bottled
- 1 to 2 tsp. Worcestershire sauce
- 1 tsp. Tabasco sauce or to your preference
- 6 to 8 tbsp. melted butter
- 1 to 2 clove garlic, minced

- 1 to 2 tbsp. vegetable oil
- ¼ tsp. salt or to taste

Cooking Directions:
1. Combine everything together (except fish and oil) in a bowl, preferably small size; mix well.
2. Arrange the fish in a shallow dish & transfer the marinade at the top.
3. Cover the dish and then place it in a fridge for a minimum period of half an hour, turning the fish after every 10 minutes.
4. Lightly coat the grill vegetable oil.
5. Remove the fish from marinade & cook for 6 to 7 minutes per side; baste the fish with the remaining marinade

Marinated Shrimp

Nutrition Info (Estimated Amount Per Serving)
30.6 Calories
10 Calories from Fat
1.2 g Total Fat
0.2 g Saturated Fat
38.2 mg Cholesterol
180.9 mg Sodium
0.5 g Total Carbohydrate
0.1 g Dietary Fiber
0.1 g Sugars
4.2 g Protein

Total Preparation & Cooking Time: 10 Minutes
Total Servings: 10

Ingredients:
- 2 pounds shrimp, medium, cooked, peeled & deveined
- 1 green onion
- 2 tbsp. olive oil
- 1 clove garlic, smashed

- 2 tbsp. fresh lemon juice
- 1 tsp. Dijon mustard
- 2 tbsp. prepared horseradish
- 1 tsp. Tobasco or hot pepper sauce
- 2 tbsp. seafood sauce or 2 tablespoons ketchup
- 1 tbsp. finely chopped chives
- Salt to taste

Cooking Directions:
1. Mix everything together (except the shrimp) in a bowl, preferably large size; mix well.
2. Add in the shrimp; toss several times to coat the shrimp with the mixture.
3. Cover & let refrigerate for several hours or overnight in a refrigerator.
4. Transfer the shrimp mixture to a serving bowl & serve with toothpicks

Marinated Cocktail Shrimp

Nutrition Info (Estimated Amount Per Serving)
73.2 Calories
8 Calories from Fat
1 g Total Fat
0.1 g Saturated Fat
119.6 mg Cholesterol
538.4 mg Sodium
1.4 g Total Carbohydrate
0 g Dietary Fiber
0.1 g Sugars
12.9 g Protein

Total Preparation & Cooking Time: 15 Minutes
Total Servings: 10

Ingredients:
- 1 pound cooked shrimp, medium, frozen & tail-on
- 3 tbsp. sherry, dry
- 2 tbsp. lime juice
- 1/4 tsp. Lawry's or Johnny's seasoning salt or to taste
- Black pepper, fresh ground to taste
- 1/4 tsp. Ancho Chile powder, dried or any chili powder, to taste
- 1/2 tsp. seafood cocktail sauce

Cooking Directions:
1. Thaw the frozen shrimp under hot running water in a colander in the sink, stirring occasionally, until separated for a minute or two.
2. Set aside and let them drain for 5 more minutes and then arrange them in a bowl, preferably large size.
3. Add the lime juice, sherry, black pepper, seasoning salt, 1/2 tsp. cocktail sauce, and Ancho powder to the bowl; stir well to coat and let rest for 10 minutes, stirring rarely.
4. Serve with your favorite cocktail sauce for dipping.

Marinated Shrimp With Capers and Dill

Nutrition Info (Estimated Amount Per Serving)
252.6 Calories
167 Calories from Fat
18.6 g Total Fat
2.6 g Saturated Fat
129.4 mg Cholesterol
298.1 mg Sodium
4.4 g Total Carbohydrate
1.3 g Dietary Fiber
0.6 g Sugars
18.1 g Protein

Total Preparation & Cooking Time: 20 Minutes
Total Servings: 08

Ingredients:
- 1 and 1/2 pounds raw shrimp, large, peeled & deveined
- 2 tbsp. Dijon mustard
- 3 tbsp. lemon juice, fresh

- 1 tbsp. lemon peel, grated
- 2 tbsp. dill, fresh & chopped
- 2 cloves garlic, large & minced
- 10 tbsp. olive oil, extra virgin
- 2 scallions, sliced thinly
- 1/4 cup nonpareil capers, drained
- 1 head of butter lettuce, leaves separated
- Pepper and salt, to taste

For Garnish
- Dill sprig, fresh
- 1 lemon, cut into rounds

Cooking Directions:
1. Over medium to high heat settings in a heavy large skillet; heat 2 tbsp. of olive oil until hot. Sprinkle shrimp with pepper and salt and then add it to the hot skillet & sauté for 3 to 4 minutes, until just opaque in the middle. Transfer the shrimp to a plate.
2. Whisk lemon juice together with the Dijon mustard, dill, garlic cloves, and lemon peel in a bowl, preferably large size. Whisk in the remaining olive oil; season with pepper and salt. Mix in the shrimp & their added juices, scallions, and capers. Cool slightly; cover and let refrigerate for a minimum period of 3 hrs or for a day.
3. Arrange the butter lettuce leaves on plates, preferably 8. Equally divide the shrimp on the plates and drizzle with additional marinade and garnish with fresh dill sprigs and lemon rounds.

Marinated Prawns

Nutrition Info (Estimated Amount Per Serving)
260.6 Calories
138 Calories from Fat
15.4 g Total Fat
2.1 g Saturated Fat
210 mg Cholesterol
949.5 mg Sodium
7.7 g Total Carbohydrate
1.8 g Dietary Fiber
2.1 g Sugars
23.7 g Protein

Total Preparation & Cooking Time: 55 Minutes
Total Servings: 04

Ingredients:
- 1 and ½ pounds green prawns, raw, peeled & deveined
- 2 lemons, juice & rind
- 3 shallots, sliced (green onions)

- 1 chili pepper, fresh, seeds removed & chopped finely
- 2 tbsp. parsley or coriander, chopped
- 3 tbsp. olive oil
- Pepper and salt to taste

Cooking Directions:
1. Arrange the prawns in a large plastic zip lock bag or shallow dish.
2. Blend all the leftover ingredients together and then transfer the mixture at top of the prawns. Turn several times to coat and let marinate for a minimum period of half an hour.
3. BBQ the prawns until cooked, for 4 to 5 minutes. Don't overcook and don't forget to baste the prawns with the marinade during the first couple of minutes of cooking time.
4. Sprinkle with some more coriander (preferably chopped), shallots or parsley with either salad or some rice. Serve & enjoy

Spicy Marinated Shrimp

Nutrition Info (Estimated Amount Per Serving)
31.5 Calories
11 Calories from Fat
1.2 g Total Fat
0.2 g Saturated Fat
38.1 mg Cholesterol
191.6 mg Sodium
0.8 g Total Carbohydrate
0.1 g Dietary Fiber
0.3 g Sugars
4.2 g Protein

Total Preparation & Cooking Time: 10 Minutes
Total Servings: 10

Ingredients:
- 2 pounds shrimp, cooked, peeled & deveined
- 1 green onion, chopped finely

- 2 tbsp. lemon juice, fresh
- 1 tsp. hot pepper sauce
- 2 tbsp. ketchup
- 1 clove garlic
- 2 tbsp. prepared horseradish
- 1 tsp. Dijon mustard
- 2 tbsp. olive oil

Cooking Directions:
1. Mix everything together (except the shrimp) in a bowl, preferably large size.
2. Add in the shrimp; toss several times to coat the shrimp with the mixture.
3. Cover; refrigerate for 4 to 6 hours or for overnight, if desired.
4. Transfer the shrimp mixture to a serving bowl & serve with toothpicks

Tamari Lemon Marinated Fish

Nutrition Info (Estimated Amount Per Serving)
408.4 Calories
93 Calories from Fat
10.3 g Total Fat
1.9 g Saturated Fat
104.3 mg Cholesterol
8228.5 mg Sodium
16.3 g Total Carbohydrate
3.6 g Dietary Fiber
5.2 g Sugars
63.3 g Protein

Total Preparation & Cooking Time: 10 Minutes
Total Servings: 02

Ingredients:
- 2 tuna, salmon, bluefish or swordfish (approximately 8 oz.)
- 1 bunch of scallion, chopped
- Juice of 1 lemon
- 1 cup tamari

Cooking Directions:
1. Combine the scallions with tamari and lemon juice.
2. Add in the fish & let marinate for half an hour or little more.
3. Preheat the grill in advance and oil it lightly; this way, you can prevent the fish from sticking.
4. Grill the fish until cooked through, basting the fish a few times with the marinade.

Red Snapper with Sesame Ginger Marinade

Nutrition Info (Estimated Amount Per Serving)
180.4 Calories
34 Calories from Fat
3.8 g Total Fat
0.7 g Saturated Fat
53.2 mg Cholesterol
568.6 mg Sodium
3.6 g Total Carbohydrate
0.8 g Dietary Fiber
0.3 g Sugars
31.5 g Protein

Total Preparation & Cooking Time: 45 Minutes
Total Servings: 04

Ingredients:
- 1 pound red snapper fillet
- 1/4 tsp. cayenne

- 1 tbsp. sesame seeds
- 2 tbsp. soy sauce
- 1 tbsp. garlic, minced
- 2 tbsp. ginger, minced
- 1 tbsp. white wine vinegar
- 1/2 tsp. sesame oil

Cooking Directions:
1. Microwave the sesame seeds for a minute, preferably over high heat settings.
2. Mix oil together with the vinegar, soy, ginger, cayenne & garlic.
3. Add in the filets & let marinade in the mixture for a minimum period of 10 to 15 minutes.
4. Arrange the filets, preferably thick side out on a plate.
5. Cover using a plastic wrap & vent in two places.
6. Microwave until thickest portion is just opaque, for 4 to 5 minutes preferably over high heat settings.
7. Let the cooked fillets stand for a couple of minutes.
8. Sprinkle toasted sesame seeds over the top.

Salmon Marinade

Nutrition Info (Estimated Amount Per Serving)
532 Calories
439 Calories from Fat
48.8 g Total Fat
6.8 g Saturated Fat
0 mg Cholesterol
7298.4 mg Sodium
13 g Total Carbohydrate
3 g Dietary Fiber
2.8 g Sugars
15 g Protein

Total Preparation & Cooking Time: 30 Minutes
Total Servings: 02

Ingredients:
- 1 pounds salmon steaks or fillets
- 1/4 lemon juice, fresh
- 1 tsp. lemon rind
- 1/3 cup soy sauce
- 2 tbsp. olive oil
- 1 tbsp. thyme, fresh & minced
- 2 cloves garlic, minced
- 1 tbsp. Italian parsley, fresh & minced

- 2 tsp. Dijon mustard
- 1 tbsp. rosemary, fresh & minced
- 2 tsp. dark sesame oil
- 1 tbsp. basil, fresh & minced

Cooking Directions:
1. Combine everything together in a large bowl.
2. Add the salmon steaks or fillet & let marinate in a refrigerator for a minimum period of an hour to 8 hrs, turning the fillets occasionally.
3. Grill, broil, or bake the Salmon until you get your desired doneness.

Grilled Salmon With Kiwi-Herb Marinade

Nutrition Info (Estimated Amount Per Serving)
722.7 Calories
423 Calories from Fat
47 g Total Fat
10 g Saturated Fat
161.5 mg Cholesterol
335.6 mg Sodium
7 g Total Carbohydrate
1.5 g Dietary Fiber
2.6 g Sugars
66 g Protein

Total Preparation & Cooking Time: 40 Minutes
Total Servings: 04

Ingredients:
- 4 salmon fillets
- 1/2 cup olive oil
- 2 tbsp. butter, melted
- 1 tbsp. Worcestershire sauce
- 2 tbsp. lime juice

- 1 kiwi, peeled & chopped
- 3 green onions, sliced
- 3 sprigs dill, fresh & chopped
- 1 to 1 and 1/2 tbsp. rosemary, dried
- 4 cloves garlic, minced
- 1 jalapeno pepper, finely chopped
- 1/4 cup cilantro, fresh & chopped
- 1 tsp. black pepper
- 2 to 3 tbsp. hickory salt, smoked

Cooking Directions:

1. Put everything together (except hickory salt and salmon fillets) in a gallon size ziplock bag or shallow dish. Using a wooden spoon; mix well until well blended. Add in the fillets and let marinate in a refrigerator for a minimum period of 4 to 8 hours.
2. Remove the fillets from marinade; when you are ready to broil or grill them; discarding the additional marinade but reserve a small amount of the marinade. Season the fillets with hickory smoked salt, preferably both sides.
3. Place the fillets on a grill, preferably hot & grill for 5 minutes. Turn and grill the other side for 5 to 7 more minutes, until salmon is done; basting the fillets with the marinade, if desired.

Honey Teriyaki Salmon

Nutrition Info (Estimated Amount Per Serving)
272.9 Calories
45 Calories from Fat
5 g Total Fat
0.9 g Saturated Fat
52.3 mg Cholesterol
2845.9 mg Sodium
28.7 g Total Carbohydrate
0.1 g Dietary Fiber
27.6 g Sugars
27.6 g Protein

Total Preparation & Cooking Time: 30 Minutes
Total Servings: 04

Ingredients:
- 1 pound salmon fillet
- 1/4 cup honey

- 1 cup teriyaki marinade or teriyaki sauce

Cooking Directions:
1. Pour everything (including the salmon) in a large zip lock bag; mix well and let the fillet marinate in the mixture for a minimum period of 4 hours, or for overnight.
2. Preheat the grill in advance, preferably over high heat settings.
3. Place the fillet on the preheated grill for 2 to 3 minutes, preferably meat side down.
4. Rotate 1/4 turn (ensure that you don't flip the fillet) & cook for 3 to 4 more minutes.
5. Flip & brush the other side with honey.
6. Cook until no longer pink, for 5 to 6 minutes

Teriyaki Tuna With Wasabi Mayonnaise & Pickled Ginger

Nutrition Info (Estimated Amount Per Serving)
148.4 Calories
105 Calories from Fat
11.7 g Total Fat
1.9 g Saturated Fat
3.8 mg Cholesterol
1484.5 mg Sodium
9.5 g Total Carbohydrate
0.1 g Dietary Fiber
5.7 g Sugars
2.3 g Protein

Total Preparation & Cooking Time: 30 Minutes
Total Servings: 04

Ingredients:
- 3 steaks of tuna, each cut into 4 strips
- 1/2 tsp. Chinese five spice powder

- 2 tbsp. pickled ginger
- ¼ cup mayonnaise
- 1 tbsp. ginger, fresh & grated
- ½ cup teriyaki marinade
- 1 tsp. wasabi paste
- 2 tbsp. peanut oil

Cooking Directions:
1. Put five spice powder together with the teriyaki marinade & ginger in a medium bowl; mix well.
2. Place the slices of tuna into a non-metallic dish.
3. Pour the mixture at the top of the marinade.
4. Cover with plastic wrap & let marinade in a refrigerator for 10 minutes.
5. Heat oil in a non-stick pan, preferably large size or use barbecue.
6. Fry tuna each side for a minute or two, preferably over moderately high heat, until cooked through to your likings.
7. Mix wasabi paste together with the mayonnaise.
8. Transfer the cooked tuna to a plate, put a small amount of the wasabi mayonnaise & finally place some pickled ginger over the top or serve it with stir-fried Chinese greens & plain, boiled rice.

Baked or Grilled Black Cod Teriyaki

Nutrition Info (Estimated Amount Per Serving)
102.2 Calories
34 Calories from Fat
3.8 g Total Fat
2.4 g Saturated Fat
10.1 mg Cholesterol
2793.7 mg Sodium
12.2 g Total Carbohydrate
0.1 g Dietary Fiber
10.2 g Sugars
4.5 g Protein

Total Preparation & Cooking Time: 30 Minutes
Total Servings: 02

Ingredients:
- 2 black cod steaks
- 1/2 cup teriyaki marinade
- 2 garlic cloves, minced
- Black pepper to taste
- 2 tsp. melted butter

Cooking Directions:
1. Preheat your oven to 175 C/350 F.
2. Mix melted butter together with a few dashes of pepper, garlic, and marinade.
3. Arrange the cod steaks, preferably in a shallow glass dish & transfer the mixture at the top of it, let marinate for a minimum period of 15 to 20 minutes.
4. Bake the fillets in a baking or casserole dish until fish flakes easily, for 25 to 30 minutes.
5. Serve the cooked steaks with white rice, preferably steamed & a small amount of the juices transferred over

Grilled Salmon Montreal

Nutrition Info (Estimated Amount Per Serving)
204.1 Calories
105 Calories from Fat
11.8 g Total Fat
1.9 g Saturated Fat
52.3 mg Cholesterol
85.6 mg Sodium
0 g Total Carbohydrate
0 g Dietary Fiber
0 g Sugars
23.3 g Protein

Total Preparation & Cooking Time: 30 Minutes
Total Servings: 02

Ingredients:
- 2 pounds salmon fillets
- 1/4 tsp. McCormick Dill Weed

- 1 package Montreal Steak Marinade, preferably McCormick Grill Mates (approximately 1 oz.)
- 1⁄4 cup water
- 2 tsp. white wine vinegar
- 1⁄4 cup olive oil

Cooking Directions:
1. Combine Marinade together with oil, water, dill weed and vinegar in bowl, preferably small size; mix well. Put the salmon in large glass dish or re-sealable plastic bag. Transfer the marinade to the bag; turn the salmon several times to coat.
2. Let marinate in a refrigerator for 15 minutes or more. Remove the salmon from marinade; discarding any leftover marinade.
3. Grill the salmon until it flakes easily with a fork, for 6 to 7 minutes per side, preferably over medium to high heat settings.

Chipotle Lime Tuna

Nutrition Info (Estimated Amount Per Serving)
224.5 Calories
111 Calories from Fat
12.4 g Total Fat
2.3 g Saturated Fat
43.1 mg Cholesterol
44.5 mg Sodium
0.3 g Total Carbohydrate
0 g Dietary Fiber
0.1 g Sugars
26.5 g Protein

Total Preparation & Cooking Time: 30 Minutes
Total Servings: 02

Ingredients:
- 2 pounds tuna steaks
- 1 package Chipotle Pepper Marinade, preferably McCormick Grill Mates (1 oz.)
- 2 tbsp. lime juice
- 1/4 cup olive oil or vegetable oil
- 1 tsp. Cilantro Leaves, preferably McCormick
- 1/4 cup water

Cooking Directions:
1. Combine Marinade together with lime juice, water, oil & cilantro in a bowl, preferably small size. Place the tuna in a glass dish or re-sealable plastic bag, preferably large size. Add the marinade to the bag with tuna; turn several times to coat well.
2. Let refrigerate for 15 minutes or little more; discarding any leftover marinade.
3. Grill until desired doneness or 5 to 6 minutes per side, preferably over medium heat settings.

Grilled Marinated Salmon Fillet

Nutrition Info (Estimated Amount Per Serving)
175 Calories
66 Calories from Fat
7.3 g Total Fat
1.1 g Saturated Fat
59.1 mg Cholesterol
487.6 mg Sodium
3 g Total Carbohydrate
0.2 g Dietary Fiber
0.5 g Sugars
23.5 g Protein

Total Preparation & Cooking Time: 30 Minutes
Total Servings: 02

Ingredients:
- 1 to 2 pound salmon fillet (Tuna or Halibut), fresh, 1" thick, rinsed & pat dry
- 3 tbsp. lemon juice, fresh

- 1 tsp. basil, fresh
- 1 tbsp. soy sauce
- 2 tbsp. garlic, minced
- 1 tsp. Worcestershire sauce
- 1/4 tsp. each black pepper & salt or to taste
- 1 tbsp. oil

Cooking Directions:
1. Mix lemon together with the Worcestershire sauce, garlic, basil, soy sauce, oil, pepper & salt in a baking pan; mix well.
2. Place the fish fillets in the mixture; turn several times to coat; cover with foil & refrigerate for half an hour.
3. Heat the grill in advance and greased the grill basket lightly; folding the thin ends to level the thickness, when you are ready to cook the fish.
4. Reserve the marinade & use it while you grill the fish.
5. Grill the fish on rack directly, preferably over medium coals until it flakes easily with a fork, for 6 to 10 minutes.
6. Baste the reserved marinade over the fillet and continue grilling until fish is flaky.
7. Garnish with fresh lemon wedges & serve with veggies, preferably grilled

Asian Marinated Grilled Tuna

Nutrition Info (Estimated Amount Per Serving)
556.6 Calories
163 Calories from Fat
18.2 g Total Fat
3.9 g Saturated Fat
86.2 mg Cholesterol
2834.9 mg Sodium
20.8 g Total Carbohydrate
1.2 g Dietary Fiber
11 g Sugars
58 g Protein

Total Preparation & Cooking Time: 02 Hrs & 30 Minutes
Total Servings: 04

Ingredients:
- 4 tuna steaks, preferably yellow fin (approximately 8 oz.)

- 1⁄3 cup sherry, dry
- 3 tbsp. ginger, chopped
- Juice of 2 lemons, fresh
- 1⁄3 cup scallion, fresh & chopped
- 2 to 3 garlic cloves, sliced
- 3 tbsp. rice wine vinegar
- 1 teriyaki sauce, bottled (10 oz)
- 2 tsp. ground pepper
- Scallion top, sliced thinly
- 2 tbsp. olive oil
- Pickled ginger

Cooking Directions:
1. Arrange the tuna steaks in a shallow dish, preferably in a single layer.
2. Combine teriyaki sauce together with the chopped scallions, chopped ginger, sherry, lemon juice, pepper, garlic, & rice wine vinegar in a large bowl; mix well.
3. Pour the mixture over the tuna steaks & let chill in a refrigerator for a couple of hours, preferably covered & turning the tuna once or twice.
4. Drain the tuna, remove from the refrigerator & allow it come to room temperature.
5. Brush olive oil all over the tuna & grill for 3 to 6 minutes on each side.
6. Serve with sliced scallions and pickled ginger.

Marinated Tuna With Cherry Sauce

Nutrition Info (Estimated Amount Per Serving)
124.4 Calories
34 Calories from Fat
3.9 g Total Fat
0.4 g Saturated Fat
0 mg Cholesterol
196.9 mg Sodium
8.6 g Total Carbohydrate
0 g Dietary Fiber
5.8 g Sugars
1.6 g Protein

Total Preparation & Cooking Time: 50 Minutes
Total Servings: 04

Ingredients:
- 6 tuna steaks (approximately 4 oz.)

For Marinade

- 1/2 cup balsamic vinegar
- 1/2 cup red wine, dry

For Sauce
- 1 tbsp. canola oil
- 1/2 tsp. sugar or sugar substitute
- 1 shallot, chopped
- 1/2 cup red wine, dry
- 1 cup vegetable or chicken broth
- 1/2 cup cherries, dried
- Salt & black pepper to taste

Cooking Directions:
1. For Marinade: Arrange the tuna steaks in a baking dish, preferably 8x8.
2. Mix wine together with the vinegar; mix well in a medium bowl & pour the mixture over the steaks in a baking dish.
3. Cover & let refrigerate for half an hour.
4. For Sauce: Over medium heat settings in a small saucepan, warm the oil & add in the shallots; cook for a minute & then add the wine, broth, sugar, and cherries; stir well.
5. Remove the fish from the marinade; drain and add it to the sauce; let the sauce to boil and then decrease the heat settings to medium-low.
6. Cook until the sauce is decreased by half, for 15 to 20 minutes.
7. Season with pepper and salt.
8. In the meantime preheat the broiler & using a non-stick spray; coat a broiler pan.
9. Put the tuna steaks on the pan & let broil until slightly pink in the middle, for 8 to 10 minutes, preferably 4" from the heat.
10. Turn the tuna over halfway through the cooking time.
11. Serve the cooked tuna with the prepared sauce.

Marinated Shrimp

Nutrition Info (Estimated Amount Per Serving)
269.2 Calories
174 Calories from Fat
19.4 g Total Fat
2.5 g Saturated Fat
143 mg Cholesterol
791.6 mg Sodium
6.9 g Total Carbohydrate
0.5 g Dietary Fiber
3.8 g Sugars
15.9 g Protein

Total Preparation & Cooking Time: 10 Minutes
Total Servings: 12

Ingredients:
- 3 pounds shrimp, unpeeled, large & raw
- 1 tbsp. hot sauce

- 2 red onions, small & sliced
- 1 yellow bell pepper
- 3 tbsp. sugar
- 1 tbsp. lemon rind, grated
- 3 tbsp. lemon juice, fresh
- 1 tbsp. white wine Worcestershire sauce
- 1/2 tsp. salt
- 1 tbsp. Dijon mustard
- 2 cloves garlic, pressed
- 1 cup vegetable oil
- 1/2 cup basil, fresh & chopped
- 1 cup red wine vinegar
- 7 and 1/2 cups water

Cooking Directions:

1. Put water in a saucepan and bring to a rolling boil, preferably over moderate heat settings. Once boiling, add in the shrimp and cook until shrimp turn pink, for 2 to 3 minutes (Don't overcook).
2. Drain & rinse with cold running water. Let the shrimp to cool in ice and then peel & devein, if desired.
3. Layer the shrimp, bell pepper slices, and red onion slices in a container, preferably airtight.
4. Whisk vegetable oil together with the remaining ingredients (except the basil); and pour the mixture over the shrimp. Cover & let chill for 2 days, stirring occasionally.
5. Just an hour before serving, add in 1/2 cup of chopped basil; stir well.

Delicious Marinated Shrimp

Nutrition Info (Estimated Amount Per Serving)
115.6 Calories
14 Calories from Fat
1.6 g Total Fat
0.2 g Saturated Fat
191 mg Cholesterol
2412.6 mg Sodium
3.7 g Total Carbohydrate
0.2 g Dietary Fiber
0.6 g Sugars
20.9 g Protein

Total Preparation & Cooking Time: 20 Minutes
Total Servings: 03

Ingredients:
- 1 pound shrimp, large, uncooked & easy peel

- 2 tbsp. cilantro, fresh & minced
- 1 clove garlic, finely chopped
- 1/2 cup water
- 1 jalapeno, medium sized, deseeded, deveined, & finely chopped
- 2 tsp. kosher salt
- 1 tsp. Old Bay Seasoning
- 4 tbsp. lime juice, fresh
- 1 tbsp. chives, fresh or dried
- 1/4 cup seafood cocktail sauce
- Water, enough to coat the fish by 1"

Cooking Directions:
1. Add water in a sauce pot, preferably medium size & place the shrimp.
2. Bring to a boil, preferably over moderate heat settings.
3. Cover & remove from heat immediately. Set the fish aside for a minute.
4. Drain & rinse the shrimp under cold running water and put into a medium bowl.
5. Cut the jalapeños lengthwise, preferably in half, devein & deseed. Place the jalapenos in the bowl with shrimp.
6. Toss with half cup of water, cilantro, lime juice, & salt to taste.
7. Cover & let refrigerate for a day.
8. Drain the shrimp, when you want to serve & toss with the Old Bay. Add crackers, preferably diverse sized & a tooth pick.
9. Put dipping sauce alongside the shrimp.
10. Sprinkle chives over the top & serve.

Tempting Marinated Shrimp

Nutrition Info (Estimated Amount Per Serving)
693.4 Calories
508 Calories from Fat
56.5 g Total Fat
7.8 g Saturated Fat
286 mg Cholesterol
1435 mg Sodium
5 g Total Carbohydrate
0.6 g Dietary Fiber
0.6 g Sugars
31.1 g Protein

Total Preparation & Cooking Time: 20 Minutes
Total Servings: 06

Ingredients:
- 2 pounds shrimp, jumbo, uncooked, peeled & deveined
- 1 cup chicken broth or white wine, dry
- 2 cloves garlic, minced

- 4 tsp. rosemary, dried & crushed
- 1/8 tsp. pepper
- 2 bay leaves
- 1 cup olive oil
- 2 tsp. oregano
- 1/4 tsp. salt

Cooking Directions:
1. Combine shrimp together with the oil, rosemary, garlic, bay leaves and oregano in a large bowl.
2. Cover & let refrigerate for a couple of hours.
3. Pour the shrimp & let marinade into a deep skillet, preferably large size.
4. Add broth or wine, pepper and salt.
5. Cover; cook until shrimp turn pink, for 10 to 15 minutes, preferably over medium to low heat settings, stirring occasionally.
6. Discard the bay leaves & transfer to a serving dish using a slotted spoon.

Spicy Marinated Shrimp & Garlic

Nutrition Info (Estimated Amount Per Serving)
455.6 Calories
336 Calories from Fat
37.3 g Total Fat
5.3 g Saturated Fat
220.9 mg Cholesterol
257.9 mg Sodium
5.8 g Total Carbohydrate
0.5 g Dietary Fiber
0.4 g Sugars
24.7 g Protein

Total Preparation & Cooking Time: 20 Minutes
Total Servings: 06

Ingredients:
- 1 and 1/2 pounds shrimp
- 30 garlic cloves, parboiled & peeled
- 1 bay leaf
- 1/2 tsp. paprika
- 1 tsp. rosemary leaf, fresh & crushed

- Parsley, fresh & chopped
- 1/4 tsp. cayenne pepper
- 1 dash of Worcestershire sauce
- Juice of 1 lemon
- 1 dash of Tabasco sauce
- Salt & pepper, fresh ground to taste
- 1 cup olive oil

Cooking Directions:
1. Over moderate heat settings in a wide & heavy skillet, gently heat the olive oil.
2. Add everything together (except parsley and the shrimp) in the skillet.
3. Gently cook for 15 minutes, stirring occasionally.
4. Increase the heat settings to high and add in the shrimp, stir well.
5. Cook until the shrimp just begin to curl and turn pink; continuously toss the shrimp in the hot oil, don't overcook else you would burn the shrimp.
6. Grate the shrimp mixture into a bowl.
7. Cover & let marinate in a refrigerator for a day.
8. Just before serving, don't forget to sprinkle with parsley.

Pepper & Vanilla-Marinated Shrimp

Nutrition Info (Estimated Amount Per Serving)
883.3 Calories
496 Calories from Fat
55.2 g Total Fat
19.4 g Saturated Fat
406.1 mg Cholesterol
954.4 mg Sodium
18.6 g Total Carbohydrate
2.5 g Dietary Fiber
6.6 g Sugars
51.5 g Protein

Total Preparation & Cooking Time: 40 Minutes
Total Servings: 02

Ingredients:
- 1 pound shrimp, medium, raw, peeled & deveined
- 1/4 cup butter, unsalted

- 1 white onion, medium, peeled & chopped finely
- 1 and 1/2 cups chicken broth
- 4 tsp. pure vanilla extract
- 1 celery stalk, chopped finely
- 3 cloves garlic, minced finely
- 1 carrot, small, peeled & chopped finely
- 2 tsp. white pepper
- 1 cup white wine, dry
- 1/4 cup olive oil

Cooking Directions:
1. Combine onion together with the carrot, garlic and celery in a large bowl, preferably non-reactive.
2. Add white pepper & 3 tsp. vanilla extract; mix well. Add in the shrimp; mix well, make sure that every piece of the shrimp is equally covered with the marinade; let marinate in a refrigerator for a minimum period of an hour to 3 hours.
3. In a skillet, preferably large size; heat butter together with the olive oil. Once the butter is melt, sauté the shrimp mixture until the shrimp turns pink on both sides. Don't forget to add the leftover 1 tsp. of vanilla extract; mix well into the pan juices.
4. Transfer the shrimp (when becoming pink) to a bowl; leaving the vegetables in the same skillet and keep aside.
5. Add the chicken broth and wine to the skillet & let simmer briskly for 15 to 20 minutes, until the sauce has thickened & the liquid has been reduced by half, stirring occasionally.
6. Briefly add in the shrimp to the sauce again & just re-heat them.
7. Serve all over cooked rice, preferably mounded.

Indian Grilled Sour Cream Marinated Shrimp

Nutrition Info (Estimated Amount Per Serving)
331.9 Calories
205 Calories from Fat
22.8 g Total Fat
13.4 g Saturated Fat
218.4 mg Cholesterol
199.5 mg Sodium
6.6 g Total Carbohydrate
0.5 g Dietary Fiber
0.3 g Sugars
25.2 g Protein

Total Preparation & Cooking Time: 03 Hrs & 20 Minutes
Total Servings: 04

Ingredients:
- 16 shrimp, jumbo, shelled & deveined

- 1 cup sour cream
- 6 cloves garlic, minced
- 1 tsp. garam masala
- 3 tbsp. butter, unsalted & melted
- 1 tsp. black peppercorns, cracked
- 4 wedges of lime, fresh for serving
- 1 tsp. cumin, ground
- 1/2 tsp. turmeric
- 1 tsp. ginger, ground
- Salt to taste

Cooking Directions:

1. Whisk sour cream together with the garam masala, cumin seeds, garlic, ground cumin, peppercorns, turmeric and ginger in a shallow dish, preferably large size.
2. Add in the shrimp & thoroughly coat with the marinade. Cover; refrigerate for a couple of hours.
3. Lightly oil your grill grates & increase the high to heat.
4. Take the shrimp out from the marinade & thread them onto the skewers; season with salt.
5. Grill the shrimp for a couple of minutes per side, until almost cooked through. Brush butter over the shrimp and grill until just cooked through and glazed.
6. Serve with fresh lime wedges.

Ginger-Soy-Lime Marinated Shrimp

Nutrition Info (Estimated Amount Per Serving)
219.4 Calories
79 Calories from Fat
8.8 g Total Fat
1.5 g Saturated Fat
172.8 mg Cholesterol
1678.2 mg Sodium
8.6 g Total Carbohydrate
0.4 g Dietary Fiber
4 g Sugars
26.3 g Protein

Total Preparation & Cooking Time: 40 Minutes
Total Servings: 08

Ingredients:

- 2 shallots, large peeled & chopped
- 1 piece of ginger, fresh, peeled & chopped (approximately 2" piece)
- 4 cloves garlic, smashed
- 3/4 cup soy sauce
- 1/2 cup lime juice, fresh
- 2 tbsp. sugar
- 1/4 cup green onion, chopped
- 1/4 cup peanut oil
- 1/4 tsp. black pepper, fresh & coarsely grounded
- 2 pounds shrimp, large, shells & tails on

Cooking Directions:

1. Place ginger together with shallots, soy, garlic, sugar, and lime juice in a high-speed blender and blend on high settings until smooth.
2. Add in the oil and green onion; blend again until well combined.
3. Season the mixture with black pepper to taste.
4. Place the shrimp in a bowl, preferably large size & transfer the marinade at the top; let marinate for 20 minutes, preferably at room temperature.
5. Preheat a grill in advance, preferably over high heat settings.
6. Remove the shrimp from marinade & grill for a couple of minutes per side.
7. If desired, serve the shrimps on paper bags, preferably brown

Sweet-N-Spicy Marinated Shrimp

Nutrition Info (Estimated Amount Per Serving)
428.7 Calories
160 Calories from Fat
17.8 g Total Fat
2.7 g Saturated Fat
345.9 mg Cholesterol
554.9 mg Sodium
19.1 g Total Carbohydrate
0.5 g Dietary Fiber
14.2 g Sugars
46.6 g Protein

Total Preparation & Cooking Time: 20 Minutes
Total Servings: 04

Ingredients:
- 1 pound shrimp, medium, uncooked & peeled
- 1/2 to 1 tsp. cayenne pepper or to taste

- 1 dash of each pepper & salt
- 2 tbsp. orange marmalade
- 1 tbsp. hoi sin sauce
- 2 tbsp. olive oil

Cooking Directions:
1. Mix olive oil together with salt, cayenne pepper, and pepper. Add in the uncooked shrimp and let marinade for a minimum period of an hour.
2. Mix hoi son sauce together with the orange marmalade.
3. Remove the shrimp from marinade & stir fry in the sauce until cooked through.

Serve immediately

Marinated Grilled Shrimp

Nutrition Info (Estimated Amount Per Serving)
246.2 Calories
98 Calories from Fat
10.9 g Total Fat
1.7 g Saturated Fat
294.5 mg Cholesterol
940.9 mg Sodium
3.6 g Total Carbohydrate
0.6 g Dietary Fiber
1.1 g Sugars
32.2 g Protein

Total Preparation & Cooking Time: 20 Minutes
Total Servings: 06

Ingredients:
- 2 pounds shrimp, peeled & deveined
- 1/4 cup parsley, fresh & minced
- 1 yellow onion, medium & diced
- 3 garlic cloves, minced
- 1 tsp. mustard, dry
- 1/4 cup basil, fresh & minced
- 2 tsp. Dijon mustard
- 1/4 tsp. pepper, ground
- Juice of 1 lemon
- 1/4 cup olive oil
- 2 tsp. kosher salt

Cooking Directions:
1. Mix everything together (including the shrimp) in a large bowl and let the shrimp to stand for a minimum period of 3 to 4 hours.
2. Grill the shrimp, preferably over moderate heat settings for 3 to 4 minutes per side.

Your Free Gift

I wanted to show my appreciation that you support my work so I've put together a free gift for you.

[TOP 10 RECIPES](http://vasilisabooks.com/freemarinadesfishbook-2/)
[Marinades , Sauces, Rubs and Glazes for meat only](http://vasilisabooks.com/freemarinadesfishbook-2/)

http://vasilisabooks.com/freemarinadesfishbook-2/

Just visit the link above to download it now.

I know you will love this gift.

Thanks!

Randy Oliver

Copyright 2016 by Randy Oliver- All rights reserved.

All rights Reserved. No part of this publication or the information in it may be quoted from or reproduced in any form by means such as printing, scanning, photocopying or otherwise without prior written permission of the copyright holder.

Disclaimer and Terms of Use: Effort has been made to ensure that the information in this book is accurate and complete, however, the author and the publisher do not warrant the accuracy of the information, text and graphics contained within the book due to the rapidly changing nature of science, research, known and unknown facts and internet. The Author and the publisher do not hold any responsibility for errors, omissions or contrary interpretation of the subject matter herein. This book is presented solely for motivational and informational purposes only.

Printed in Great Britain
by Amazon